GILDA
BERGER

EASTER AND OTHER SPRING HOLIDAYS

FRANKLIN WATTS
New York / London / Toronto / Sydney / 1983
A FIRST BOOK

Illustrations by Anne Canevari Green

Photographs courtesy of
the Religious News Service:
opp. p. 1, pp. 15, 16, 30, and 37;
the New York Public Library
Picture Collection: pp. 4 and 48;
the Greater New Orleans Tourist
& Convention Commission: p. 25;
Bill Fitz-Patrick/The White House: p. 42.

Library of Congress Cataloging in Publication Data

Berger, Gilda.
Easter and other spring holidays.

(A First book)
Includes index.
Summary: Describes the origins and ways of
celebrating festivals and holidays marking
spring around the world in various religions,
but emphasizing Easter particularly. Includes
some Easter handicrafts, games, and recipes.
1. Easter—Juvenile literature.
2. Spring—Folklore—Juvenile literature.
[1. Easter. 2. Spring.] I. Title.
JUV GT4935.B47 1983.   394.2'68283   82-17616
ISBN 0-531-04547-1

CONTENTS

ONE
Origins of the Spring Holidays
1

TWO
The Jewish Festivals
10

THREE
The Story of Easter
19

FOUR
The Days Before Easter
22

FIVE
Holy Week and Easter Sunday
27

SIX
Seven Weeks After Easter
35

SEVEN
Holiday Customs
39

EIGHT
Holiday Projects
46

NINE
Party Fun
57

Index
64

EASTER AND OTHER SPRING HOLIDAYS

1

ORIGINS OF THE SPRING HOLIDAYS

Spring holidays have been celebrated at least since the beginning of recorded history. They mark the end of winter, a time when all the earth seems dead, and the start of the spring season, when everything appears to come to life again.

The seasons change because of the earth's tilt as it rotates on its axis. Spring arrives when the earth is tilted so that the sun is directly over the equator.

In the northern parts of the world, the first day of spring is on or about March 21. This is the day of the vernal equinox. The word *vernal* means "spring"; *equinox* means "equal night." Night and day are the same length on the first day of spring. Each lasts exactly twelve hours.

Long before people celebrated Easter or any other modern spring holiday, they connected spring with the return of life to the earth. They noticed that at the end of winter, buds and tiny green leaves began to appear on bare branches. Flowers poked up through the ground in woods and fields. Many frogs left their holes and traveled to water to lay their eggs. Woodchucks and other hibernating animals came out of their underground burrows and looked around for something to eat. Migrating birds returned, built nests, and laid eggs.

The return of spring was an even bigger event to ancient peoples than it is to us. It meant that they could be free of worrying how to stay warm inside their unheated dwellings. After the inevitable food shortages of winter, they could hunt the plentiful game once more and plant their spring crops.

Early peoples had no idea what caused the change of seasons. They believed each of the various forces of nature was ruled by an individual god, a being far more powerful than themselves. These mythical beings were regarded with fear and awe. The people sought to please the gods in order to assure their own survival.

Dwellers in the northern and central parts of Europe had a deity whom they called Eostre, goddess of spring. Her name is thought to have come from the word used to describe the direction of the sunrise—"east." The word *Easter*, some think, was derived from this same source.

Every spring, the people in these lands welcomed the return of warmth to their region by holding a festival to honor and thank Eostre. They offered the goddess special cakes that they baked for the festival. These cakes were very much like the hot cross buns that we have today.

Some early tribes believed that things found in nature, such as stones, rivers, trees, and mountains, had their own spirits. Many think that the May Day festival started as a tree-worshiping rite. The ancient Druids, a pre-Christian religious sect found mostly in Britain and France, thought that trees, and oak trees in particular, were sacred objects. The Druids prayed to the trees for sunshine, rain, and to make the earth fertile.

For many centuries, people went into the woods early on the morning of May 1, or May Day. They cut down branches of trees, brought them home, and hung them over their windows and doorways. Sometimes they would cut down a tall, straight tree instead, which they would then carry around town, bringing good luck to all the houses. They would then place the tree in the center of the village, where people would dance around it and honor it.

Today, especially in Britain, May Day is celebrated with a dance around a tall Maypole. Each dancer holds the end of a long, gaily colored ribbon that is attached to the top of the pole. As the dancers move around the pole, the ribbons intertwine and form a beautiful design that eventually covers the pole.

The ancient Greeks believed that the gods held sway not only over the lives of individuals but also over the powerful forces of nature. They tended to revere the gods of the sun and moon, for example, rather than spirits thought to live in such objects as trees.

The ancient Greeks created a story to explain the change of seasons. It involved Demeter, goddess of the earth and agriculture, and Persephone, her beautiful daughter. One day, while Persephone was gathering flowers in a meadow, the earth opened up in front of her. The god Hades, king of the underworld, appeared in his black chariot. He seized Persephone and carried her off to his kingdom deep inside the earth to make her his bride.

Demeter was grief-stricken at the disappearance of her daughter. She searched everywhere but could find no trace of her. She became so sad and disheartened that she stopped doing her work. All the plants on earth withered and died. Nothing new would grow.

The other gods felt sorry for humans and begged Demeter to mend her ways. She refused. At last she was told by Apollo, the god of the sun, what had happened to Persephone. Demeter went to Zeus, king of the gods, and demanded that her daughter be returned to her.

Persephone, meanwhile, had refused to eat any food as long as she was kept prisoner in the underworld. She knew that once a soul, human or divine, ate food in the lower region, he or she was doomed to spend all eternity there. So Hades sent his servants to the earth above to bring back something tempting for Persephone to eat. They brought back seeds of the pomegranate fruit.

Hades deceived Persephone by telling her that it was safe to eat seeds, as they were not really food. Persephone, growing weak from hunger, ate one.

Now Zeus knew of Hades' deception and also of Persephone's mistake in having eaten the seed. So he told Demeter that her daughter would have to remain in the lower world for half of each year from that day forth. This is wintertime on earth. It is the season when Demeter will not let anything grow. She is gloomy because her daughter is with Hades. But every spring, Persephone is allowed to return to her mother. Then, Demeter makes the earth come alive again because she is joyful to have her daughter back.

May Day celebrations almost always include a Maypole dance, in which dancers wind brightly colored ribbons around a tree or tall pole.

The Celts, who lived mostly in Great Britain in ancient times, had a May Day celebration for their sun god. They believed that this god was held prisoner all winter by the evil spirits of cold and darkness. Each year, around the first of May, the god escaped and brought sunlight and warmth back to the earth.

To help the sun escape, the Celts lit giant bonfires on the highest hills in their villages. This was to frighten away the evil spirits and force them to free the sun. To this day, traditions such as lighting special fires and burning candles continue to be part of spring celebrations in many lands.

Most early Europeans believed in evil spirits. Some thought that the night before May Day was an especially dangerous time. This was when witches and goblins gathered, they said. The Germans believed, for instance, that all the evil witches flew up to peaks in the Harz Mountains on their broomsticks every spring. On their way, the witches would torment anyone they could catch.

The villagers lit fires, blew horns, shouted, and used noise-makers to frighten away the goblins. They also prayed for protection against evil.

Much later in history, the evening before May Day became known as Walpurgis Night. People called on St. Walpurga, an eighth-century saint, to save them. Although few people today believe that witches or evil spirits gather the night before May Day, some Danes, Norwegians, and Swedes still build huge bonfires on Walpurgis Night. The Germans who live in the Harz mountain area still parade through the streets carrying witches made of straw. Later they burn the straw witches in honor of St. Walpurga.

Another May Day celebration also comes from the time when people believed in nature gods. Over 2,000 years ago, the

Romans worshiped Flora, the goddess of flowering plants. They believed Flora made the flowers bloom each spring.

To be sure that Flora returned every year, they honored her with a festival called Floralia. The celebration lasted six days, from April 28 to May 3. During Floralia, people gathered spring flowers and prepared offerings to Flora. Each day of the festival, feasts, parades, dancing, sports events, and plays were held in her honor. One of the most important contests was a footrace for young men. Each contestant tried to be first to place his wreath on Flora's statue. The winner was then thought to be assured of good luck for the following year.

Buddhists have long been celebrating spring with merry-making and gaiety. The name of the festival varies. For example, in Sri Lanka it is called *Wesak*; in Thailand, it is known by the name of *Visakha Puja*. Both are usually held during the month of May to commemorate the birth, enlightenment, and death of the prophet Buddha, founder of the Buddhist religion. People decorate their homes and temples with paper lanterns and attend special services in the temples.

The Japanese celebrate the birthday of Buddha on April 8, in a festival called *Kambutsue*. During *Kambutsue*, small, flower-covered shrines are erected over statues of the infant Buddha. The worshipers then pour sweet, specially prepared scented tea over the statues. Because of the flower decorations and the closeness of the date to the start of the cherry blossom season, *Kambutsue* is also known as Flower Day.

A national holiday in Japan, *Shumbun-no-hi* comes on the day of the vernal equinox and is intended to celebrate nature and all growing things. One event of the day is a visit to the family cemetery. The purpose is not to mourn the dead but to experience happy thoughts and feelings about them. Usually a meal is eaten at the cemetery, with traditional picnic foods such as soft rice balls (*o-hagi*) and tossed vegetables with chopped seafood (*naze-sushi*) being served.

Hindus celebrate the three-day festival of *Holi* during the month of March. The holy festival began as a sacrifice to ensure good crops. One version of the custom dates back to an ancient legend about a witch named Holika. This witch had done so much harm that the people decided to burn her at the stake. To make sure that other witches would not hear her shrieks and try to save her, the people made lots of noise. They shouted and sang. The angriest ones threw things at Holika.

Still, some worried that Holika might be able to do evil after her death. So, as an offering, they threw dates and fried beans into the fire for Holika to eat.

In our own time, on the night before *Holi*, a pot filled with beans and water is placed in a hole in the ground. Over it, a giant bonfire is lit. The villagers walk slowly around the blazing fire, yelling and cursing. At the same time, they toss coconuts, dates, and fried beans into the fire. The ashes that remain are considered sacred and are sometimes buried in the fields to improve the crops.

During *Holi* each family prepares a number of special dishes. People then go from house to house, visiting, exchanging gifts, and tasting the various dishes. The host will usually mark the foreheads of the guests with a dab of colored powder.

Meanwhile, out in the street, the children are busy making mischief. Often, they will fill bamboo tubes with colored powder and blow the powder over friends or anyone else who comes along. They will load toy pistols with red-tinted water and squirt the water at anyone unlucky enough to come within range. People of all ages throw handfuls of mud at each other.

April Fools' Day, the first day of April, is traditionally a time for playing harmless jokes or tricks on others. Some believe this practice began in India and grew out of the *Holi* celebration.

Others think it began in France, about four hundred years ago. It started, they say, after the French king, Charles IX, adopted the new Gregorian calendar, making January 1 New Year's Day. Until then, March 25 had marked the beginning of the new year, and the people had celebrated its arrival from March 25 until April 1.

According to legend, there were many who did not like the change and thus kept observing New Year's Day on April 1. These people came to be known as April fools. It became the custom to fool friends on that day. One old trick was to give someone a joke-present, such as a candy box filled with straw or a bouquet of onions instead of flowers. In France, victims of April fool jokes are called April fish; in Scotland, they are known as April gowks.

When settlers came to America from Europe, they brought the notion of April Fools' Day with them. The tradition of playing pranks on one another on the first day of April has continued ever since.

How do you and your family celebrate spring? With flowers? With ceremonies or specially prepared foods? With worship? With fun and games? No matter the way, you are sure to find it has some connection with the past. Let's look now at some modern Jewish festivals that celebrate spring in ways that can be traced back thousands of years.

2

THE JEWISH FESTIVALS

Spring celebrations are an old and very important part of the Jewish tradition. The festivals have both seasonal and historical meanings. Wherever Jews live, they mark the beginning of spring with the holidays *Tu b'Shevat*, Purim, and Passover.

TU B'SHEVAT—
NEW YEAR FOR TREES

Around March, when the sap begins to flow again in the trees, Jews celebrate the holiday known as *Tu b'Shevat*, or New Year for Trees. It is dated 15 *Shevat* in the Hebrew calendar.

Historically, *Tu b'Shevat* is a sort of birthday party for trees. In ancient times it told the people whether the fruit of the tree, which according to Jewish law could not be eaten until the fourth year, was ready to be picked. It was also used to tell the age of the tree for purposes of setting its value.

The tree has always been an important symbol in the Jewish religion. For some, it represents the Tree of Life and stands for all that is noble and worthwhile. In addition, the flow of the sap in the trees is taken as a symbol of the continual stream of God's blessings throughout nature.

A number of customs are associated with *Tu b'Shevat*. One is to eat the fruit of the trees, especially those that are native to the land of Israel, such as dates, figs, raisins, nuts, and St. John's bread. Another is to stay up most or all of the night studying or reciting passages from the Hebrew Bible and other sacred writings that have to do with fruit and trees. Between periods of study, the scholars eat the fruits they have read about. Doing this plus reciting the correct prayers, it is believed, keeps the divine blessings flowing in the world.

In recent years, *Tu b'Shevat* has become a kind of Arbor Day in Israel. Many Jews living in other countries contribute money for the planting of trees in the Holy Land. It is customary, too, for Israeli children to go to the fields and plant trees. The tree ceremony is always followed by dancing, singing, and other festivities.

PURIM—
THE FEAST OF LOTS

The Jewish feast of Purim, held in early spring, marks the rescue of the Jews from a cruel plot that threatened to destroy them. It is held on the 14th day of *Adar* in the Hebrew calendar. The holiday is apparently historical in origin. Yet it resembles the folk holidays held at the beginning of spring in many other cultures.

The story of Purim is told in the part of the Bible known as the Book of Esther, or the *megillah*. It explains how, in 600 B.C., the wicked Haman, prime minister of Persia (now Iran), became angry at Mordecai, a Jew, for refusing to pay him homage. Haman convinced King Ahasuerus to grant him authority to kill all the Jews in the land. As a way of choosing the best day for his plan, Haman cast lots. The name of the festival, Purim, comes from the Hebrew words for "lots."

Queen Esther, the beautiful Jewish girl who had married the king, and Mordecai, who was her cousin, hatched a plan to save the Jews and expose Haman for the wicked man he was. Risking the king's anger, Queen Esther was able to persuade him to allow the Jews to be warned of the massacre. As a result of this warning, many Jews survived the intended slaughter. Not long after, Haman was hung for treason.

Jews commemorate the event with great joy and feasting. The day usually begins with a service in which the rabbi reads the *megillah*. Every time the name of Haman is mentioned, though, listeners drown it out with noisemakers. The traditional instrument is the *grager*. You can buy a *grager* in a toy store or make one at home by taking two aluminum foil pie plates and putting a handful of hard beans or pebbles between them. Seal the rims with staples, and paint a design on the outsides of the plates. Now hold the rim of your homemade *grager* with two hands, and shake it up and down to create the noise.

If you want an even noisier *grager*, fill an empty coffee can with pebbles or nails. Decorate the can, cover it with a tight plastic lid, and shake hard every time Haman's name is mentioned.

Usually, coins are collected before the service or prior to the *megillah* reading. This is a reminder of the tax collected in biblical times to support the temple. The money is usually given to charity. Also customary during this time of good feeling is to give *shalkhmones,* which are presents of fruit, cookies, and candy, to the poor and to at least one friend.

Families often gather together in the afternoon for a Purim feast. Hamentaschen, which are three-cornered poppy-seed, prune, or apricot-filled cookies that symbolize the three-cornered hat Haman is believed to have worn, are usually served. Children dress up in costumes to look like Queen Esther, her cousin Mordecai, King Ahasuerus, and the wicked Haman. Often they attend parties or take part in a Purim play that re-enacts the story of Esther.

Here is a simple recipe for hamentaschen:

2 cups flour
1½ tsp. baking powder
6 tbsp. sugar
pinch of salt
2 eggs, beaten
3 tbsp. salad oil
prune or apricot butter

Sift the dry ingredients together. Make a hole in the center and add the eggs and oil. Mix thoroughly.

Roll out the dough to a ⅛-inch (.31-cm) thickness on a lightly floured board. Cut into rounds about 3 inches (7.5 cm) each in diameter. Place a tablespoon of prune or apricot butter on each round.

Now bring three edges of each circle together to form a triangular-shaped cookie. Bake on a greased cookie sheet in a 350° oven until golden brown (about 30 minutes). This recipe makes about 30 small hamentaschen.

PASSOVER

One of the major festivals of the Jewish people is called Passover. The name comes from the last plague that God brought on the ancient Egyptians. According to the story, the Egyptian pharaoh refused to free the enslaved Jews even after Moses told him that God had ordered it. As punishment for the pharaoh's stubbornness, God caused nine terrible plagues to descend on the Egyptians.

The plagues, though, served only to harden the will of the pharaoh. So God ordered the tenth plague. He sent the Angel of Death to kill the eldest son of each household, but told him to "pass over" the homes of the Israelites, marked by the blood of a paschal (newborn) lamb. This made the pharaoh relent, and he ordered Moses to take the Israelites and lead them out of Egypt at once.

Passover is also known as *Pesach*, a Hebrew word referring to the ancient spring festival *Hag ha-Pesach*, or the Festival of the Paschal Sacrifice. The paschal sacrifice was the offering made by shepherds of the first lamb born in the spring. At the same time, there was the holiday *Hag ha-Matzot*, or Festival of the Matzoh. This name comes from the offering of grain made by the farmers in those times.

All three events—the exodus of the Jews from slavery in Egypt and the ancient festivals of *Pesach* and *Matzot*—occurred at the same time of the year. Soon the paschal sacrifice became connected with the meal that God commanded the Israelites to eat the evening before they left Egypt. And the word *matzoh* came to be identified with the flat, unleavened bread that the

The festival of Passover is associated with the Paschal sacrifice, in which the first lamb born in the spring was slain by shepherds as an offering to God. Contemporary American artist Leonard Baskin did this watercolor.

In this painting by Arthur Szyk, the ceremonial
Passover meal, called a seder, is depicted.

Jews ate on their hasty flight out of Egypt, since they had no time to wait for the dough to rise as usual.

According to tradition, Passover begins on the 15th day of *Nisan* in the Hebrew calendar. To prepare for the holiday, the family removes all leavened breads and cakes from the house. They take out and wash special dishes, flatware, and cookware that will be used only for Passover.

On the night of Passover, the entire family sits down to a traditional meal known as the seder. Ideally, members of several generations are present. Each has a part to play. The word *seder* means "order," because a certain order is always followed in observing the ritual.

Everything to do with the seder is explained in a small book called the Haggadah. At most seders, each family member has a copy of the Haggadah to read from and to follow. The Haggadah retells the story of the exodus and discusses the religious and historical meaning of Passover.

It is customary to invite to the seder the poor and those without their own family seders to attend. In fact, as part of the seder, the door is opened and a cup of wine is prepared for the prophet Elijah. Legend has it that Elijah will arrive dressed as a poor beggar to test whether or not the world is ready for the Messiah, or deliverer of the Jewish people.

The seder plate, which is placed in the center of the table or near the head of the house, perhaps best explains the seasonal and historical meanings of the occasion. It contains the following symbols of the rebirth and renewal of the Jewish people:

Matzoh—a reminder of the unleavened bread the Israelites ate during their exodus from Egypt.

Roasted shankbone—a symbol of the paschal sacrifice the ancients brought to the temple.

Roasted egg—a symbol of the burnt offerings Jews once took to the temple; it may also symbolize in part their new life after release from slavery.

Bitter herbs—a token of the bitterness of slavery in Egypt.

Haroset—a mixture of nuts and apples that symbolizes the mortar used by the Jews in building structures for the pharaoh.

Parsley and saltwater—the parsley is a symbol of the arrival of spring and the return of green plants to the earth. The saltwater represents either the tears shed by the Hebrew slaves or the Red Sea, which parted to allow the Hebrews to escape from Egypt.

Four cups of wine—symbols of God's four-part promise of redemption, or salvation: "I will bring you forth; I will deliver you; I will redeem you; I will take you."

The seder always ends with the singing of *Chad Gadya*, "An Only Kid." This is a folk song about a father who bought a kid, or little goat, for two *zuzim*, two small ancient coins. The kid is eaten by the cat, who is bitten by the dog, which is beaten by a stick, which is burned by the fire, which is quenched by the water, which is drunk by the ox, who is slaughtered by the *shohet* (ritual butcher), who is killed by death's angel, who is destroyed by the Holy One.

According to one interpretation, the kid symbolizes the Jewish people. The song then refers to the many conquerors of the Jews who were defeated in turn by others. It ends with the hope that God will one day do away with all oppressors so that the world will become a truly joyous place in which to live.

Orthodox Jews observe Passover for eight days, while other Jews observe it for seven. For all Jewish people, though, the first two days are considered the most significant.

3

THE STORY
OF EASTER

Easter is a Christian holiday that is based on the biblical account of the death and resurrection, or rising from the dead, of Jesus Christ. But it relates to many other spring festivals as well, because it also commemorates nature's awakening and rebirth.

Jesus, who was born a Jew, lived about 2,000 years ago in Judea. At the time of Jesus' birth, this area was one of the Roman provinces. Today it is part of the modern state of Israel. As a young man, Jesus began to preach a new religious message. He taught about the Kingdom of God and said that he had the power to forgive sins.

Most leaders in the community distrusted and feared Jesus because he wanted to change many of the old and accepted practices of the time. Several groups considered him a dangerous and revolutionary figure who wanted to stir up the masses against Rome.

One of the most detailed accounts of the last week of Jesus' life on earth is found in Gospels, the Book of Matthew, Chapters 21 through 28. It begins with the arrival of Jesus in Jerusalem on Sunday to celebrate the Jewish holiday of Passover. Jesus made a triumphal entry into the city riding on an ass. Large crowds gathered to greet and cheer him. They cut down branches of palm trees and placed them in his path.

Jesus' first act in Jerusalem was to go into the temple and drive out the merchants. He believed that the House of God was to be used for worship only, not for making money. Over the next few days, he prayed, preached, and told the people of his special mission on earth, saying that he had been sent down by God, his father, to save others by giving his own life.

On Thursday night, the Bible relates, Jesus attended a Passover seder with his twelve disciples. During the meal, which is now called the Last Supper, Jesus announced to his disciples that one of them would betray him. Later that night, Jesus went to a garden on the Mount of Olives to pray. While there, a group of Roman soldiers came and arrested him. One of his disciples, Judas Iscariot, had indeed betrayed him by pointing him out to the soldiers for the reward of thirty pieces of silver.

Jesus was brought before a court of Jewish elders. They accused him of breaking God's laws by calling himself the Son of God and King of the Jews. Since Judea was under Roman rule, the elders sent Jesus to the Roman governor, Pontius Pilate, for trial.

The next day, Friday, Jesus was tried and found guilty of the crime of treason against the state. He was sentenced to death by crucifixion, an especially cruel punishment in which the victim is nailed to a cross and left to die. Crucifixion was used by the Romans only for slaves and the worst criminals.

The Roman soldiers who carried out the sentence made fun of Jesus. They made him wear a red blanket and pretended it was a royal robe. They put a crown of thorns on his head and mockingly called him King of the Jews. Jesus was forced to carry his own cross to a hill outside Jerusalem, called Golgotha or Calvary. Here he was crucified.

That Friday, after three hours on the cross, Jesus died. One of his followers, Joseph of Arimathea, took down the body and placed it in a tomb that had been carved in rock. Joseph then rolled a heavy stone in front to block the entrance. Because Jesus had said he would rise from his grave, Pilate sent soldiers to seal the tomb and make sure that no one removed the body.

Three days later, though, on Sunday, when Jesus' followers went to the tomb, they found it empty. They looked on this as the fulfillment of the prophecy Jesus had made that he would rise up from the dead. And it is this event, the resurrection of the Christ, that is celebrated on Easter Sunday.

In the early days of the Christian Church, up until A.D. 325, followers observed Easter at the same time as the Jewish Passover. In fact, the name for Easter in several languages comes from *Pesach*, the Hebrew word for Passover. In Spanish, for example, Easter is *Pascua*; in French, *Pâques*; in Italian, *Pasqua*; in Dutch, *Pasen*; in Swedish, *Påsk*; and in Albanian, *Pashkë*.

4

THE DAYS
BEFORE EASTER

Easter does not have a fixed date. It falls on a different day each year, depending on the time of the full moon in March. It is set as the first Sunday after the first full moon on or after March 21. Therefore, Easter always comes between March 22 and April 25.

Before Easter begins, there is a forty-day period of fasting and self-denial called Lent. The name *Lent* comes from the old Anglo-Saxon word, *lencten*, meaning "spring." It is a time when Christians prepare for Easter by not eating certain foods. They also do penance for sins they have committed, give alms, avoid amusements, and refrain from entering into marriages.

Over the centuries, the length of Lent has varied, and the strictness of the fast has changed. One of the earliest records shows that in the second century Lent lasted just forty hours, from the afternoon of Good Friday to Easter Sunday morning. During that time, the faithful were forbidden to take any food or drink.

Gradually, the length of the Lenten season grew. Now it is forty days, starting on Ash Wednesday and ending on Easter

Sunday. The total number of days is actually more than forty because the count excludes Sundays.

The forty-day period is thought to be a symbol for the forty days Jesus fasted in the wilderness before he began to preach. The forty-hour fast may have originated from the belief that Jesus was in the tomb from Friday afternoon to Sunday morning.

Lent is observed by all branches of Christianity. Most Protestant churches hold special services or meetings to honor the Lenten season. But in Roman Catholic churches, a special mass is held each day. The priests wear purple robes that are reserved especially for these services.

SHROVE TUESDAY

The final day before Lent begins is called Shrove Tuesday. Its name comes from the old custom of being shriven, or confessing, on that day.

The day is also called Pancake Tuesday by some. The reason for this name is that at one time people were not allowed to eat eggs, butter, or milk during Lent. Making stacks and stacks of pancakes was a good way of using up these foods.

The French call Shrove Tuesday Mardi Gras. *Mardi Gras* literally means "fat Tuesday." It refers to the old practice by the French of parading a very fat ox through the streets of their towns on this day.

The French introduced the Mardi Gras to America around the year 1766. Instead of pancakes, Mardi Gras is celebrated with carnivals and parties. The custom of rejoicing before Lent caught on wherever the French settled. The practice of having a carnival before a period of fast dates back even further, to ancient Roman times.

The most outstanding Mardi Gras celebration in America is held each year in New Orleans, Louisiana. During the carnival season, about two weeks before Lent, a king and queen of Mardi Gras are chosen. Various societies organize balls and parties. On Tuesday, Mardi Gras day, large numbers of marching bands and people in fanciful costumes hold a parade. Elaborate floats pass down main streets. From these floats, the people toss souvenirs, such as strings of inexpensive beads, to the onlookers. The parade is big, noisy, crowded, and very gay.

ASH WEDNESDAY

Ash Wednesday, which comes the day after Shrove Tuesday, marks the start of Lent. It recalls the old custom, followed by kings, of covering the head with ashes to show that one is sorry for any wrongs committed.

In the churches of many countries, the priest makes a cross of ashes on the forehead of the faithful, saying, "Remember, man, that thou art dust, and unto dust thou shalt return."

The ashes are a symbol of penance, of regret for one's sins. They are made from the palms or branches that were used in church on Palm Sunday of the previous year. The palms are burned and blessed in preparation for Ash Wednesday.

On Ash Wednesday in New Orleans there is a tradition of "burying the sardine." Actually, a thin slice of meat, not a sardine, is buried in the ground. This serves as a reminder of the fast that is beginning.

THE FOURTH SUNDAY

The fourth Sunday of Lent comes near the midway point of the holiday. It is an especially joyous day and is called Laetare Sunday.

The French celebrate Mardi Gras, or "Fat Tuesday,"
by parading a fat ox through the streets. In the
United States, Mardi Gras is celebrated with
carnivals and parties in New Orleans, Louisiana.

In the past, the pope would carry a golden rose in his hand while celebrating mass on that day. Originally, the pope held a single rose. Since the fifteenth century, though, he has carried a bouquet of roses made of gold set with precious jewels.

In England, the fourth Sunday is also known as Mothering Sunday. It is celebrated in very much the same way as Mother's Day in the United States. Mothering Sunday began as a tradition of allowing young or unmarried servants to return to their homes before Easter, so they could attend services at the church where they grew up. As part of the observance, the young people would place gifts in front of the church altar. Over the years, the meaning of Mothering Sunday has been extended. Now all young people are expected to bring gifts to their mothers and to be especially helpful around the house on that day.

Of the entire period of Lent, the final week, called Holy Week, is of the greatest importance in the Easter celebration. In the next chapter we'll look at what happens during Holy Week.

5

HOLY WEEK
AND
EASTER SUNDAY

The week before Easter is called Holy Week. It starts with Palm Sunday. The Monday, Tuesday, and Wednesday of that week are not major feast days. Then comes Maundy Thursday, Good Friday, and Holy Saturday. At the end of Holy Week is Easter Sunday, to many the most important day of the Christian year.

PALM SUNDAY

Palm Sunday marks the day Jesus rode triumphantly into Jerusalem on an ass. The day takes its name from the fact that people spread branches of date palm and olive trees on the ground before him and waved palm leaves in greeting.

In some churches, palm leaves are brought in, and the priests bless crosses made of them. The palm crosses are handed out to worshipers at the end of the service. Other times just the building is decorated with the leaves. Sometimes, people form the blessed palm leaves into small crosses and wear them in their hatbands or buttonholes.

The Roman Catholic celebration of Palm Sunday almost always includes a solemn church procession. The church faithful carry palms or substitutes such as olive branches or shoots of pussy willow. During the special mass, the congregation chants the Gospel story of the crucifixion of Jesus.

Some of the most elaborate processions are held in Spain, Mexico, and various Latin American countries. People there carry huge statues of Jesus and his mother, the Virgin Mary, through the streets. Sometimes it takes over thirty men to carry one statue. Other marchers include men with hoods over their heads or chains tied to their feet.

Local customs for Palm Sunday differ around the world. In Rapallo, Italy, for instance, trays of silkworms are brought to church to be blessed. Young girls in northern Greece carry beautifully embroidered handkerchiefs and sing Easter songs. Mexican villagers carry to church large crosses that they have decorated with fruits and cakes.

One ancient custom that has not been lost is that of giving the church a special cleaning for Palm Sunday. In some places, dirt swept up from the church floor is scattered in the fields in the belief that it will insure good crops. Some say that the annual ritual of housecleaning at springtime came from this Palm Sunday rite.

MAUNDY THURSDAY

Thursday of Holy Week is called Maundy Thursday. It is also sometimes known as Holy Thursday. On this day, Christians recall the last meal that Jesus ate with his disciples.

The name *Maundy* probably comes from the Latin *mandatum,* or commandment. It has to do with the message Christ brought to his disciples: "A new commandment I give unto you: that ye love one another." Before he gave them this commandment, it is said, Jesus washed their feet to show his devotion to helping and serving others.

To this day on Maundy Thursday, many priests and ministers wash the feet of twelve worshipers, one for each disciple. The popes carried on this tradition at St. Peter's in Rome until 1878. After a long interruption, the practice was begun again in 1961 and has continued to today.

In some churches, the cross is covered with a white veil on this day. The church bells, which ring throughout the service, are then silenced until Saturday morning. Some believe that this is in respect for Jesus' agony on the cross. Children in several countries are told that "the bells have gone to Rome," and that they will bring eggs with them on their return.

GOOD FRIDAY

Good Friday, for the Christian world, is a reminder of the day Jesus died on the cross. The name itself probably comes from the earlier name, God's Friday. In many lands it is a national holiday. For the faithful, it is a day rigorously observed by fasting and attending church services.

Although the particular form of worship varies from church to church, some parts of the service are the same almost everywhere. The retelling of the story of the crucifixion of Christ is nearly universal, for example. So is the three-hour service, which traditionally lasts from noon until three o'clock.

The Stations of the Cross is a rite found mostly in Roman Catholic churches. These churches have pictures or carvings of the various events on the day of Jesus' crucifixion. The places in the church where the pictures are located are called stations.

Worshipers walk from one station to another, praying or meditating. They progress from the sentence of death to the burial of Jesus. There are fourteen stations in all.

In some countries, special customs have become part of Good Friday observances. In Greece, for example, life-size statues of figures involved in the death of Christ are carried through the streets in a procession that often lasts for several hours. Then the marchers return to the church, where a priest blesses candles and gives them out.

It is customary in Italy for young boys to beat the church pews with willow branches on Good Friday. This is a symbolic thrashing of Judas, the disciple who betrayed Jesus.

A few Good Friday traditions have little religious or historical significance. Clothes washed on Good Friday, some people claim, will become spotty, and bread baked on that day will never get moldy. People catch the rain that falls, believing that it can be used to cure eye diseases.

HOLY SATURDAY

Holy Saturday is generally a time of rest in the religious observances of Holy Week. Some churches, however, do hold services. A special vigil on Holy Saturday night may end with

After being found guilty of treason,
Jesus was sentenced to death
by crucifixion. This painting,
entitled "Crucifixion," is by Italian
artist Parri Spinello (1387–1453).

mass at midnight. Also, the day is favored by some as a good time for baptisms.

One devotional act on this day is the blessing of the Easter fire. Outside the church, the priest or other church official strikes metal against a flint. From the resulting spark a flame is lit. Some say that this represents the coming of light into the world with the resurrection of Jesus, but it is also almost definitely linked to the ancient tradition of celebrating the longer hours of daylight in springtime.

The new fire is brought into the church. It is then used to relight all the candles and sanctuary lights.

In Germany and Austria, Holy Saturday is celebrated with processions. Bands parade through the streets in Italy, followed by children shaking rattles and noisemakers. At one time, the mothers stayed at home striking the doors with wooden sticks to drive out the devil.

The Mexican custom for Holy Saturday is called "the burning of Judas." Large paper dolls of Judas are made and stuffed with firecrackers. Coins are tied to the outside. Then, while thousands watch, the figures are thrown into the streets, and the firecrackers are exploded.

EASTER SUNDAY

Easter Sunday is the climax of the entire celebration of Easter. The faithful believe that Jesus was resurrected on this day, that he rose up from the dead. Easter church services are especially beautiful and usually include some glorious music written to commemorate the occasion.

In colonial days in America, the church ceremonies on Easter Sunday were very simple. The reason was that many of the early settlers were Puritans, who believed that religious observances should be pure and plain.

Usually, churches are specially decorated for the holiday. White is the principal color used. There are also flower displays, most often featuring the Easter lily. Few types of native American lilies bloom before early summer. Therefore, the early-blooming Bermuda lily, with its striking white, trumpet-shaped blossom, is imported and is now widely accepted in the United States as the Easter lily.

One of the favorite customs on Easter Sunday is the dawn, or sunrise, service. In many places around the United States, thousands gather for outdoor worship before the sun comes up. Perhaps best known is the ceremony held at the Hollywood Bowl in California, where crowds of up to 30,000 gather to await the sunrise.

There are several possible explanations on how the tradition of dawn services began. One is that Jesus' tomb was found empty at dawn. Another is related to the ancient belief that the sun could actually be seen dancing in the sky at dawn on the first day of spring. And finally, the custom might in some way be associated with the huge fires that people lit on the night before the vernal equinox.

Whether services are held outdoors at dawn or indoors later in the morning, almost every Christian goes to church on Easter Sunday. People generally dress in new spring clothes. The custom of wearing new apparel started with the ancient belief that the earth put on new garments in springtime. It was considered lucky to wear something new at spring festivals.

When church services are over, many stroll in the Easter Parade. The Easter Parade is not a parade in the usual sense of the word. It is mostly a chance to stroll around, see what everyone is wearing, and be seen. Perhaps the most well-known Easter Parade takes place along New York City's Fifth Avenue, near St. Patrick's Cathedral. Many streets along the avenue are closed to traffic, and the event is shown on television.

Afterward, people get together with friends and family for Easter dinner. The main dish is usually ham, turkey, or lamb. Wine is served with the meal, and fancy cakes are eaten for dessert.

Each country has its own particular customs for Easter Day. In Poland, where the holiday is called *Wielkanoc*, the head of the house cuts up a colored egg at the Easter dinner. Everyone at the table gets a piece. The family greets each other by saying, "We wish you a happy alleluia."

When the family returns home from church in Switzerland, the parents call the children in to show them what the Easter bunny has brought. Usually there are gifts of chocolate rabbits and candy eggs. Portuguese children are given sugarcoated almonds of many different colors wrapped in folded pieces of paper. And in Spain, it is customary to spend Easter afternoon watching the bullfights.

6

SEVEN WEEKS AFTER EASTER

A special week in the spring, important to both Christians and Jews, starts seven weeks after Easter and Passover. Jews celebrate *Shavuot*, the Feast of Weeks, which includes the Festival of the Harvest and the Festival of the First Fruits. Christians celebrate Pentecost, or Whitsunday. This is the birthday of the church and celebrates the beginning of the spread of Christianity.

SHAVUOT

Like Passover, *Shavuot* has both seasonal and historical origins. The holiday comes fifty days after Passover. It marks the end of the grain harvest. This was the time when people brought the first fruits of the season to Mount Zion.

The holiday also marks the birth of the Jewish religion. According to tradition, Moses stood on top of Mount Sinai on this day and received the Torah, containing the Ten Commandments, from God. From then on, Israel became a nation whose mission was to observe the Law that God had commanded.

It is customary on the two-day festival of *Shavuot* to decorate both the home and synagogue with branches, greens, and flowers. Some congregations spread grass on the floor of the synagogue. This is to represent the grass on which the people of Israel stood while receiving the Torah.

The traditional observance of *Shavuot* has become more solemn over the years. It sometimes involves staying up all night, studying and discussing the Torah. It is said that the heavens open up at midnight on *Shavuot*, making it a good time for sending up prayers.

In olden times, people brought offerings of two loaves of bread, freshly baked using wheat from the new crop, to the temple. All during the growing season, families would come to the temple with their offerings of thanksgiving. In our own time, twin loaves of bread are baked and served to the family.

Mostly dairy foods are eaten during *Shavuot*. A great favorite are blintzes, which are thin pancakes rolled around a filling of cheese, potato, or fruit. The reason for serving simple foods is to leave more time for the contemplation of the Torah.

PENTECOST OR WHITSUNTIDE

According to the New Testament, Christ's disciples were gathered to celebrate the Jewish Festival, the Feast of Weeks. From the heavens above them appeared tongues of fire. At that

*These Israeli children are carrying
the first fruits of the harvest
as part of the* **Shavuot** *celebration.*

moment, the disciples were suddenly able to speak many foreign languages. This helped them go forth and preach Christianity to the rest of the world.

Pentecost is the Greek word for *Shavuot*. The word literally means "fiftieth." The name was chosen because the holiday falls on the fiftieth day after Passover. The British call Pentecost Whitsunday. The reason for this was that new Christians were often baptized during Pentecost. They wore white robes during the ceremony, giving the holiday the name White Sunday. In time, this became shortened to Whitsunday. All Christian churches celebrate Holy Communion and Confirmation on this occasion.

In some countries, especially in the northern regions, where spring comes late, the Pentecost celebration has more to do with the change in season than with religion. People decorate their churches and cathedrals with flowers. In Denmark, for example, where Pentecost is called *Pinse*, it is a joyous spring festival. On the morning of *Pinse*, many Danes awaken early to see the sunrise. They dance and celebrate the long-awaited coming of spring to their land. Families go to the country and take along picnic lunches. They gather branches from beech trees that are about to bloom and later decorate their homes with them.

The dove, a symbol of the Holy Spirit, is widely used to represent Pentecost. At one time doves were set free in churches during Pentecost services. In modern days, churches sometimes suspend a painted dove over the altar. Families may hang pictures of doves in their kitchens or dining rooms.

7

HOLIDAY CUSTOMS

Almost all Easter customs or traditions can be traced back to the early festivals celebrating nature's rebirth in the spring. Many stem from the Greeks or other peoples in the ancient world. Even though many of these groups became Christian, they kept a number of their own customs. Gradually, the different ways of observing the spring holiday were combined to become the rich mixture of symbols, beliefs, and activities that is Easter today.

EGGS

The oldest of all spring customs is that of giving and receiving eggs. The egg has universally symbolized the return of life to the world in springtime.

Early peoples such as the Persians, among others, thought the world was hatched from an enormous egg. The Chinese used eggs as temple offerings.

Many ancient tribes ate colored eggs during their spring festivals. They also gave them as gifts. The colors used to paint the eggs were originally made from vegetables and flowers. Even when people began to create their own dyes, they tried to retain the wonderful colors of nature.

Eggs have long been a part of the Jewish tradition. Jews eat eggs on many important occasions. One of the foods on the seder plate for the Jewish Passover is a roasted egg. The most common explanation is that the egg represents the burnt offerings made at the temple at major festivals. Since it is a symbol of life, however, it may also be a reminder of the hope for salvation and the new life the Jews began after their release from slavery in Egypt.

The custom might have come from the Romans (or even earlier, from the Greeks), who often prepared roasted eggs. The seder also usually starts with a hard-boiled egg dipped in salt-water. This, too, was possibly borrowed from the Romans, who considered it lucky to begin a meal with an egg. Records show that by the fourth century, still early in the history of Christianity, eggs were already part of the Easter tradition. For Christians, the egg meant hope and resurrection.

In Greece, people used to dye eggs red. Red was thought to be a magical color. Breaking the shell of the red eggs, the Greeks believed, let the blessing escape. Some eggs were colored red to symbolize Jesus' bleeding on the cross. Today the Greeks dye eggs all different colors and use them in a special Easter greeting. When two people meet at Eastertime they hold out their eggs and tap them lightly together. One says, "Christ is risen." The other answers, "He is risen indeed."

In Sweden and other Scandanavian countries there are always eggs on the table on Easter morning. Everyone tries to eat as many as possible. The Danes like to eat hard-boiled eggs dipped in mustard sauce.

In Italy and some other European countries, people eat

Easter breads baked with eggs embedded in them. One historian believes that this practice comes from an ancient magic rite in which offerings of bread assured prosperity to the family.

Egg rolling at Easter is another ancient tradition still popular in several countries. Children roll eggs down a grassy slope. The idea is to see whose egg gets to the bottom first.

For many years, the best-known egg rolling in the United States took place in Washington, D.C., at the White House, on the Monday after Easter. But for the last several years, egg hunts have been held instead. Adults must be accompanied by a child to be admitted. Thousands of children hunt Easter eggs on the White House lawn. Prizes are given to those who win the contests.

The first egg-rolling contests were probably part of the athletic competitions that took place during pagan spring festivals. Over the ages, though, the custom of egg rolling also grew to symbolize the rolling away of the stone from Jesus' tomb on the morning of his resurrection.

In many countries it is the custom for children to awaken early on Easter Day and hunt for eggs that their parents have hidden. The eggs are sometimes placed in special baskets that the children leave. They are told that the eggs are brought by the Easter rabbit.

RABBIT

The symbol of the Easter rabbit is most commonly believed to have come from the association most people made between rabbits and fertility. In ancient Egypt, the rabbit represented birth and new life.

To some ancient peoples, the rabbit was considered a symbol of the moon. Some historians think the bunny became a

*In past years, on Easter Sunday, children
would gather on the White House lawn to take part
in an annual egg-rolling contest.*

symbol of Easter because the exact date of the holy day depends on the movements of the moon. Others say it is part of Easter because long ago people considered the rabbit a sacred animal. It is thought that hares were sacrificed to the goddess Eostre.

Few consider the rabbit a sacred creature any longer. But many young children are taught to believe that the Easter bunny brings eggs at Easter.

LAMB

The tradition of eating lamb as a special Easter treat dates back to pagan times when animals were offered as sacrifices. When animals were no longer actually sacrificed, a symbol was substituted.

The Bible tells how the ancient Israelites sacrificed newborn lambs as a tribute to God. Today, the shankbone of a lamb is part of the seder plate. It is a reminder of the paschal sacrifice the ancients brought to Solomon's Temple in Jerusalem.

Many Christians believe the lamb symbolizes the sacrifice of Jesus, who died for the good of all people. They eat the paschal lamb at Easter. It may be roasted on a spit, as in Greece, or prepared in many other ways.

CANDLES, LIGHTS, AND BONFIRES

Fire ceremonies of many sorts were used at the pagan spring festivals. Today, in many parts of northern and central Europe, people light huge bonfires on the hilltops at Easter. Then they gather around the fires and sing Easter hymns. Others explode fireworks at Easter. In parts of Sweden, the children dress up as witches at Easter. Fireworks are then set off to frighten them away.

An impressive fire ceremony takes place in Jerusalem every year on Holy Thursday. Fifty churchmen carrying banners and singing songs parade around the tomb of Christ in the center of the Church of the Holy Sepulcher. Then the bells ring out. A fire is lit, and flames shoot out through openings in the church wall. Thousands of people move toward the fires to light candles they have brought with them. The inside of the huge church soon becomes a glittering display of lights.

It used to be the custom in some countries to put out the church candles and lights on Good Friday. Then, on the night before Easter, the priest would light the main candle, called the Paschal candle, with new fire. This candle would then be used to relight all the candles in the church. The worshipers would light their own candles from the great Paschal candle. On Easter morning in France, it is still traditional for people to take home candles that have been blessed at church. They use these candles only on special occasions. It is expected that the candles will last until the following Easter.

The tradition of blessing a very large candle at Easter was mentioned in early Christian writings. Some candles blessed on Easter evening and used after Easter contain five grains of incense, for the five wounds that Jesus received during his crucifixion.

PROCESSIONS

Processions, or marches, are very much a part of Easter in many lands. In certain localities, such processions may have originally been connected with fertility rites.

While most processions are held on Palm Sunday, in some places, such as in the city of Seville in Spain, there are processions each evening during Holy Week. Men, hidden under curtains that hang from the bottom of huge platforms, carry very large statues of Jesus and the Virgin Mary past the thousands of onlookers who line the streets.

In Jerusalem, the devout follow the road Jesus walked to his place of execution. This path is called the *Via Dolorosa,* which means "sorrowful road."

Processions in which the viewers wear masks are a traditional feature of pre-Lent festivals in some lands such as Germany and Austria. In one version, on Shrove Tuesday, masked boys lead a group of youngsters from house to house. They beg for gifts and collect sausages and eggs. In one Middle-European village, the dancers in the procession are showered with hempseed. In response to this, they jump as high as they can. This is supposed to help the hemp plants grow tall.

8

HOLIDAY PROJECTS

NATURAL DYES

Coloring or decorating eggs for Easter can be fun. Some people buy dyes of many colors in a store. But the traditional way is to prepare dyes from materials that you have at home.

One of the oldest vegetable dyes is made from the dry, papery outer skins of ordinary onions. The skins make a pretty yellow dye. Here is how to proceed:

1. Peel the dry skin from several onions. The more skins you use, the darker the dye will be.
2. Put the skins in a pan and cover them with cold water.
3. Boil them for 5 to 10 minutes.
4. Strain the liquid dye into a bowl and throw away the skins.
5. Add 1 tablespoon of vinegar to the dye to "fix" the color and make it permanent.

Other vegetables, such as spinach and beets, can be used to make dyes of other colors. They can be prepared in the same way as the onion-skin dye. The spinach dye will be a light green. The beet produces a reddish color. Strong tea, made with ordinary tea leaves or tea bags, is another natural dye. The color is a mixture of red and gold.

Once you have made dyes of different colors, you are ready to decorate the eggs.

HARD-BOILED EGGS

Hard-boiled eggs are often used for decorating. The eggs are prepared the same way as any eggs to be sliced or chopped. Place the eggs in a pan and cover them with water. Boil for 15 minutes. Drain off the water, and allow the eggs to cool.

You can make patterns on the eggs by placing a cutout of whatever shape you like on the eggs before you paint them or by putting masking tape on them before they are dipped in dye. Remove the cutout or the tape after the color is dry.

You can also color or make pictures on the hard-boiled egg with crayons, paint, or felt-tip markers. To make the egg even more attractive, you may want to make it glossy by putting a coat of varnish over it.

First varnish just the top part of the egg and let it dry. Then varnish the bottom part. Warning: Eggs that have been varnished are NOT safe to eat.

EASTER CHICK

1. Take a hard-boiled egg and dye it yellow.
2. Fold a piece of yellow paper in half. Cut a beak, tail, pair of wings, and two feet.
3. Glue the parts on the egg.
4. With a felt-tip pen draw in the two eyes.

HOLLOW EGGS

To make a hollow egg, you must blow out the contents. The yolk and white can later be used to make omelets, cakes, or anything else that requires eggs.

Here is how to make a hollow egg:

1. Keep some fresh eggs at room temperature for a few hours.
2. Shake the egg back and forth vigorously, to loosen the yolk and make it easier to blow out.
3. Make a hole in the bigger end with a needle or pin. Wiggle the needle around in the hole to make it a little larger.
4. In the same way, make another, smaller hole in the small end.
5. Hold your lips over the second hole and blow the egg out through the bigger hole and into a bowl.
6. Wash the shell and stand it on end to dry.

THE EGG TREE

In Germany, people prepare a number of hollow eggs before Easter. First, they color them. Then they use them to make "egg trees."

These intricate designs are some traditional Ukrainian patterns you can trace and use to create your own colored Easter eggs. Please don't cut them out of the book, however.

To color the eggs:
1. Place the clean, blown egg into a bowl of dye.
2. Leave it there until it turns as dark as you want it to be.
3. Drain, and put it on a paper towel to dry.
4. Rub the egg with a little vegetable oil to make it shiny.
5. Glue yarn, feathers, sequins, beads, or paper cutouts on the egg for decoration. Or, make designs with paint or felt-tip marking pens.

To make the egg tree:
1. Collect a number of branches from a willow or birch tree.
2. Glue or tape one end of a short length of thread to each blown-out colored egg. Then attach the eggs to the branches with the free ends of the thread. If you wish, you may also add ribbons and small pretzels to the branches.
3. Stand the egg tree in a pretty vase.

EASTER TWIGS

At Easter the Swedes decorate small birch branches and twigs with colored feathers. You can follow this same tradition:
1. Find a few branches with buds that are about to open.
2. Obtain some feathers from an old feather pillow.
3. Dye the feathers using different colored inks. (Do not use paint, or the feathers will get sticky.) Let them dry on a paper towel.
4. Using thread, attach the feathers to the twigs.
5. Put the twigs in water and wait for the leaves to open up.

FORCED BRANCHES

To get a head start on spring, you can force branches to bloom:

1. Bring some forsythia, pussy willow, lilac, peach, apple, cherry, or crabapple branches into the house as soon as the first buds appear.
2. Put them into a vase filled partway with water. With proper planning, you can have a beautiful arrangement of branches in bloom in time for Easter or Passover. Making arrangements with these forced branches is an attractive and inexpensive way to decorate your home. It is also a lovely gift to give someone else.

FORCED BULBS

Forcing makes flowers bloom ahead of when they normally would outdoors:
1. Buy a few bulbs in a garden shop early in the autumn. Crocuses, daffodils, and hyacinths are good choices.
2. Put the bulbs in a bowl with sand or loose soil.
3. Leave them in a closet or other dark place for about two months. Keep the soil moist but not too wet.
4. As soon as you see some green shoots poking up, the bulbs should be brought into a bright room. Add a little water daily.
5. The first bulbs to bloom will be snowdrops and crocuses. Daffodils and hyacinths come later.

SPRING FLOWERS

Early in spring, but before the ground is warm, you can start seedlings indoors in eggshells. Then, when the weather is warm, they will be a good size for planting outside. Here is how to proceed:
1. Save up about a dozen empty eggshells (broken ones, not blown-out ones). Put them into an egg carton.

2. Fill the shells with dirt. Place a seed of nasturtium or other spring flower in each shell and cover with more dirt.
3. Water daily.
4. When the weather is warm and your plant is a few inches (5 cm) tall, you are ready to plant it outside. Poke a few holes in the bottom of the shells. Then just set them into the ground, eggshells and all.

WINDOWSILL GARDEN

You can make a tiny garden of different plants for your windowsill this way:
1. Fill the cups of an old muffin tin with dirt.
2. Plant several seeds in each cup. Use a variety of seeds.
3. Give the seeds a little water each day.
4. Pull out the plants that are not growing well. Leave only the two healthiest plants growing in each cup.

EASTER HATS

In some towns and cities, there is a contest for the best hat or bonnet worn in the Easter Parade. Often, people wear hats they have made themselves. Here are some basic directions for making a top hat and a bonnet.

To make the top hat:
1. Cut a large strip of construction paper about 6 inches (15 cm) wide.
2. Wrap the paper around your head. Tape or staple the cylinder together to keep the shape.
3. Place the cylinder on the center of another piece of construction paper. Trace around the outside of the cylinder.

4. Lift the cylinder and cut out the circle you have just drawn. The circle will be the top of the hat.
5. Round the corners of the piece of paper from which you cut the circle. This will become the brim.
6. Cut six 2-inch (5-cm) slits in top and bottom of cylinder.
7. Slide the cylinder through the round opening in the brim. Fold the flaps out, and glue the brim to the flaps.
8. Fold the top flaps in. Glue the top in place.
9. Paint a bright design on your top hat. Glue on a feather or two if you wish.

To make a bonnet:
1. Get a 12-inch (30-cm) paper plate.
2. Straighten one side by drawing a 9-inch (22.5-cm) line from edge to edge. Cut along the line.
3. Cut 2-inch (5-cm) slits all around the curved edge of the paper plate.
4. Fit a 12-inch-wide (30-cm) strip of construction paper, wallpaper, or gift wrapping around the curved edge. Fold the flaps in, and glue this paper to the flaps.
5. Poke holes through the bottom two edges of the paper. Attach a 12-inch (30-cm) length of colorful ribbon to each hole.
6. Paint your bonnet or decorate it with small tissue flowers.

BUNNY SOCK

What better gift for Easter than a handmade rabbit doll? All you need is a torn, but clean, thick white sock and some cotton or other material for stuffing.

1. Cut 4 inches (10 cm) off the toe. Save the toe. Lay the sock flat.

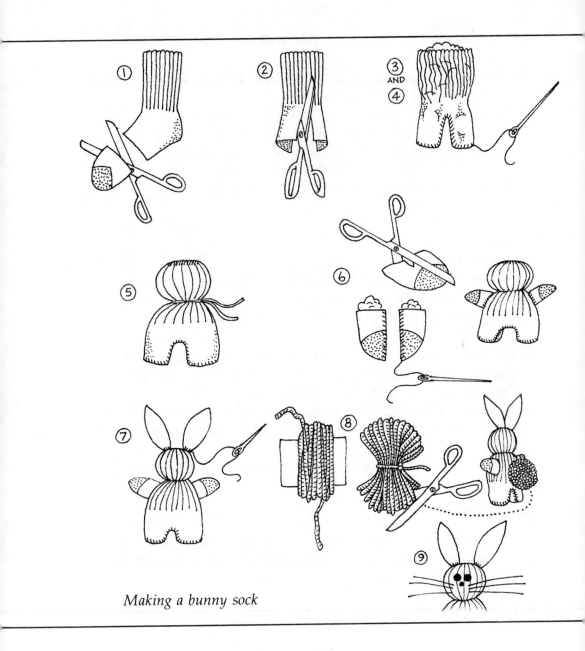

Making a bunny sock

2. Cut through the middle of the remaining part of the foot section of the sock. The two parts will be the bunny's two legs.
3. Sew each leg together, and stuff with cotton or other material.
4. Stuff the rest of the bunny's body.
5. Tie a string near the top to make the neck and head.
6. Cut the cut-off toe section in half. Sew the ends together and stuff. Sew the toe section on the sides of the bunny to represent its paws.
7. Cut out two stiff cardboard ears. Attach them to the body using needle and thread.
8. Make a tail by winding yarn around a 2-inch (5-cm) piece of cardboard fifty times. Then tie it in the middle and cut both ends. Sew this to the heel of the sock.
9. Either glue or sew on felt (or button) eyes, a nose, and whiskers.

FLOWER BOUQUET

A pretty bouquet of paper flowers is fun to make and a nice gift, too. Here is how to make one:

1. Hold a glass, rim down, on a piece of colored tissue paper. Draw a circle around the glass. Draw as many circles as you can fit on the piece of paper.
2. Cut out the circles.
3. Make a stack of three circles as the petals for one flower. Shape all three petals by cutting curves or fringes around the edges.
4. Poke a pin through the center of the three petals.
5. Hold the pin against a piece of wire such as the kind used to

hang pictures. Wrap colored tape around the pin and wire. Place the flower in a vase.

6. Prepare other flowers with different colored tissue, and with a mixture of colors. Make them different sizes and different shapes. Use varying lengths of wire.

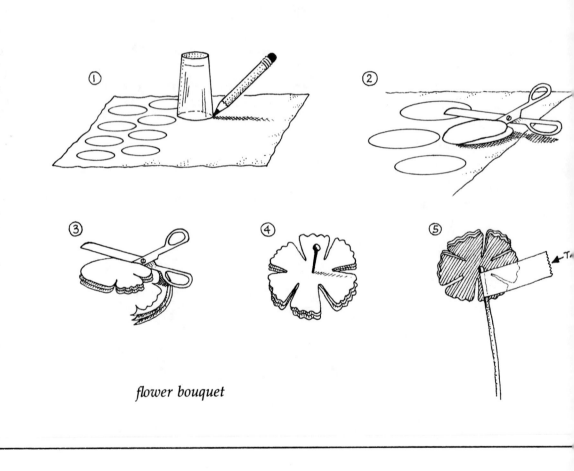

flower bouquet

9

PARTY
FUN

Getting together with friends and family at Easter is part of the joy of the holiday season. In different countries people have traditional games they play and foods they eat at Easter parties or other spring get-togethers. Many of the games are really contests, producing winners and losers. Some believe that having these competitions is a tradition left over from the ancient spring rituals.

EASTER GAMES

Almost every Easter party starts with an egg hunt. Before the party gets under way, hide a number of hard-boiled eggs (or jelly beans) around the inside or outside of the house. When everyone is present, hand each person an Easter basket (such as the bunny basket below), and send them to hunt for eggs. The one who finds the most eggs receives a prize.

The following "bunny basket" can be used for collecting eggs on an egg hunt. At the end of the party, it can also be filled with candy as a gift for the guests.

1. Collect enough empty quart-size milk cartons for all of the guests. Wash and dry them thoroughly.
2. Have an adult use a sharp knife to cut off the bottom 4 inches (10 cm) of each container. This will be the basket.
3. Decorate the basket by covering it, inside and out, with aluminum foil. Or, cut out a piece of gift wrap or shelving paper to fit, and paste it around the inside and outside.
4. Outline and cut out a 6-inch-tall (15-cm) bunny with a round head, round body, and two long ears. Draw in eyes, nose, and mouth.
5. Glue or staple a bunny to each side of the basket.

For the Greek Egg-Tapping Game, each player is given a colored hard-boiled egg. The object is to see who has the strongest egg. The one with the last egg to break is the winner.

Players hold the eggs in their hands so that only the small end is showing. Then the first two players tap the small ends together. The idea is to hit hard enough to crack the other player's egg but not so hard that your own eggshell cracks. Each time an egg is broken, the winner plays someone new. Losers eat their eggs. The game goes on until all the eggs are cracked. If an egg remains unbroken through Easter, some believe it is a sign of good luck for the coming year.

The German Egg-Blowing Game requires at least one blown egg. (See Chapter 8 on how to prepare a blown egg.)

Place the egg in the center of a flat, clean table. The guests at the party all gather around the table. One person gets the game under way by blowing the egg across the table to the opposite side. The person closest to the egg now blows it back. No one can touch the egg. Anyone who lets the egg fall off the table has to leave the game. The last person to remain wins the prize.

Players stand in a circle to play the French Egg-Passing Game, a variation of a game of egg tossing. Each person is given a soup spoon. One player gets a hard-boiled egg and places it on the spoon.

The game starts when the player who has the egg passes it to the spoon of the person on the right. If the egg falls, the person on the right must leave the circle. Otherwise, the egg is passed on to the next person on the right. The game continues until only one person remains. That person is the winner.

To play the Russian Egg-Rolling Game, you need a clear floor area. Begin the game by rolling a colored hard-boiled egg toward the center of the floor. That egg is the target egg.

Each player, in turn, tries to roll his or her egg toward the target. The object of the game is to land as close as possible to it. It is all right if one egg bumps another egg and lands near the target. The winner is the player whose egg is closest to the target after everyone has had a turn. Repeat the game five times to find the champion.

EASTER EATS

The party table should reflect the twin themes of Easter and spring. Place cards, showing each guest where to sit, can help set the mood. Here is a simple way to make some place cards:

1. Take a blank sheet of paper. (Ordinary typing paper will be fine.)
2. Fold it neatly in half so that it can stand by itself.
3. Use paint, a felt-tip pen, or crayons to show grass growing on the bottom of one side of the card.
4. On top of the grass write the guest's name.
5. Around the name draw some Easter bunnies and color them in.

6. Take little puffs of cotton or make small balls out of white tissue paper and glue them in place for bunny tails.

Place a minted fruit cup at each person's place. The green and gold colors are a reminder of spring.

To make the fruit cup, cut up some oranges, grapefruit, and pineapple. If you like, you can buy them already sliced in cans or jars. Add some crushed mint leaves to a cup of orange juice. Pour the juice over the fruit. Serve cold.

Stuffed eggs are a wonderful way to use up all the extra hard-boiled eggs at the party. You will need:

6 hard-boiled eggs
2 tbsp. mayonnaise
1 tsp. vinegar
1 tsp. mustard
1/2 tsp. salt
dash of pepper
1/4 tsp. paprika

Peel the eggs and cut them in half lengthwise. Carefully remove the yolks and put them into a small bowl. Set the whites aside until later. Mash the yolks. Stir in the mayonnaise, vinegar, mustard, salt, freshly ground pepper, and paprika.

Stir until smooth. Spoon the yolks into the whites. Place on a bed of lettuce, with a slice of tomato on the side.

For a different main dish, you can use the eggs you blew out (see Chapter 8) to make hollow eggs for egg-in-bun sandwiches. You will need:

4 eggs
4 hamburger buns

1 stick butter or margarine
4 slices of cheese to be melted

Set the oven at 325°. Cut into the bun 1 inch (2.5 cm) or so with a biscuit cutter or a small juice glass, but *do not cut through the bottom of the bun.* Carefully lift out the circle with a fork. Butter the inside of the buns, and place them on a cookie sheet. Pour one egg into each hole. Sprinkle with salt and pepper. Bake in the oven for 25 minutes. Top with the cheese and bake 5 more minutes.

No party is complete without a decorated Easter cake.

First, use any standard recipe or mix to bake a yellow cake. Frost it with white frosting and tint it yellow with yellow food coloring.

Now make bunny decorations for the cake for each guest (or as many as will fit nicely on the cake). Here is how to make the bunnies:

1. Use a toothpick to fasten two marshmallows together for the bunny's head and body.
2. Cut a marshmallow into quarters.
3. Use a piece of toothpick to fasten one quarter on each bunny for a tail.
4. Cut bunny ears from pink construction paper.
5. Poke the ears into the top marshmallow of each bunny.
6. Dip a toothpick in red food coloring and draw the eyes and a smiling mouth.
7. Dip another toothpick in yellow food coloring and add yellow whiskers.
8. Arrange the bunny decorations around the top of the cake.

Bunny decorations for the cake

The following Easter cookies can be passed around the table on a platter or individually wrapped as party favors. To make about 30 delicious cookies you will need:

1 cup butter or margarine
1½ cups sugar
3 eggs
3 cups sifted flour
3 tsp. baking powder
1 tbsp. milk
2 tsp. vanilla

Cream the butter and sugar. Add the eggs and beat well. Sift the dry ingredients and add them to the creamed mixture. Now add the milk and the vanilla, and chill the dough for 1 hour.

Roll out the dough until it is about ¼-inch (.625-cm) thick. Dip a rabbit-shaped cookie cutter into flour and cut the cookies. Put them on a greased baking sheet, and bake for 15 minutes at 350°.

INDEX

April Fool's Day, 9
Arbor Day, 11
Ash Wednesday, 22, 24

Bitter herbs, 18
Bonfires, 43–44
"Burning of Judas," 32
"Burying the sardine," 24

Candles, lights, and bonfires,
   43–44
Chad Gadya, 18
"Crucifixion," 30
Customs, 39–45

Dove as symbol, 38
Druids, 2

Easter, 19–21

pre-Easter, 22–26
Easter Sunday, 27–34
after Easter, 35–38
Easter cake, 61, 62
Easter chick project, 47
Easter clothes, 33
Easter cookies, 63
Easter dinner, 34
Easter eggs, 48. *See also* Eggs
Easter fire, 32
Easter food, 59–63
Easter hats, 52–53
Easter lilies, 33
Easter Parade, 33
Easter Sunday, 27–34, 42
Easter twigs, 50
Egg hunt, 41, 57–58
Egg rolling, 41, 42, 59
Egg tree, 49–50

Eggs
    coloring and decorating,
      46–47
    hard-boiled, 47
    hollow, 49
    roasted, 18, 40
    stuffed, 60
    as symbols, 39–41

Fat Tuesday, 25
Feast of Lots, 10–13
Feast of Weeks, 35, 36, 38
Festival of the First Fruits, 35
Festival of the Harvest, 35
Festival of the Matzoh, 14
Festival of the Paschal Sacri-
    fice, 14
Fireworks, 43–44
Flower bouquet, 56
Flower Day, 7
Flowers, forcing, 50–51
Fourth Sunday, 24, 26

Games, 57–59
Golgotha, 21
Good Friday, 29, 31
Grager, 12

Hag ha-Matzot, 14
Hag ha-Pesach, 14
Haggadah, 17
Haman, 11–12

Hamentaschen, 12–13
Haroset, 18
Holi Festival, 8
Holiday customs, 39–45
Holiday projects, 46–56
Holy Saturday, 31–32
Holy Thursday, 28–29, 44
Holy Week, 26–34
Hot cross buns, 2

Jewish festivals, 10–18, 36
Jewish religion, birth of,
    35

Kambatsue, 7

Laetare Sunday, 24, 26
Lamb as symbol, 43
Last Supper, 20
Lent, 22

Mardi Gras, 23–25
Matzoh, 14, 17
Maunday Thursday, 27–29
May Day, 2, 3, 4, 6
Maypole, 3, 4
Megillah, 11–12
Mothering Sunday, 26
Mythology, 3–5

Nature gods, 6–7
Nisan, 17

Palm Sunday, 27–28
Pancake Tuesday, 23
Paschal candle, 44
Paschal lamb, 43
Passover, 10, 13–18, 20, 21, 40
Pentecost, 35, 36, 38
Pesach, 14, 21
Pinse, 38
Place cards, 59
Processions, 44–45
Projects, Easter, 46–56
Purim, 10–13

Rabbit, as symbol, 41, 43
Rabbit doll, 53, 55

Seder, 17, 20, 40
Shalkhmones, 12
Shankbone (roasted), 17
Shavuot, 35–37
"Shriven," 23
Shrove Tuesday, 23–24, 45

Shumbun-no-hi, 7
Spring flowers, 51–52
Spring holidays, origins of, 1–9
Spring housecleaning, 28
Stations of the Cross, 29, 31
Sunrise Easter service, 33

Torah, 35
Tree of Life, 10
Tu b'Shevat, 10–11

Ukrainian Easter eggs, 48

Vernal equinox, 1, 33
Via Dolorosa, 45
Visakha Puja, 7

Walpurgis Night, 6
Wesak, 7
Whitsuntide, 35, 36, 38
Wielkanoc, 34
Windowsill garden, 52